Degrees of Reading Power®, DRP®, and DRP→BookLink® are registered trademarks
of Touchstone Applied Science Associates, Inc.

Text layout and design by Kim Harris
Cover design by Becky Malone
Production Assistance by Denise Geddis

ISBN 1-57035-232-1

Printed in the United States of America

Published and Distributed by

Sopris West
*Helping You Meet the Needs
of At-Risk Students*

4093 Specialty Place • Longmont, CO 80504 • (303) 651-2829
www.sopriswest.com

Contents

Unit 7

Map

CONCEPTS & CONTENT	NOTES & EXAMPLES

READING

❏ The **past tense** of a verb can sound like /t/, /d/, or /ed/.

❏ The plural ending **s** can sound like /s/, /z/, or /es/.

❏ Phoneme-grapheme correspondences in this unit:
  - **qu** sounds like /kw/
  - The sound combination /kw/ is spelled with **qu** almost all the time
  - **x** sounds like /ks/
  - The sound sequence /ks/ is the only two-phoneme combination that can be spelled with one letter, **x**
  - Sometimes **s** sounds like /z/.

❏ The letters **y** and **z** represent single consonant sounds. The letters **qu** and **x** each represent two phonemes.

SPELLING

❏ Meaning determines spelling, as in the **homophones** sax and sacks.

❏ **Comprehension** questions require interpretation or translation of information. Some words signal a Comprehension question: **define in your own words**; **explain**; **tell**; **paraphrase**.

❏ Stories have different parts. The **initiating event** in a story describes the problem or situation to which the characters respond.

ACTIVITIES, ASSIGNMENTS & ASSESSMENT

❏ Fluency Builders   1   2   3   4

❏ Reading Assignment: *J & J Language Readers* Unit 7, Book 1: *The Rat Pack*; Book 2: *Max Zaps the Can*; Book 3: *The Quick Fix*

❏ Independent Reading: _____

_____

_____

Mastery Tasks   1   2   3   4
                      ❏   ❏   ❏   ❏

CONCEPTS & CONTENT	NOTES & EXAMPLES

❑ Six Traits of Effective Writing:
Focus: Word Choice

    A strong verb makes a good sentence.

❑ **Verbs** are words that describe action.

❑ Verb endings can tell about the time of the action:
- To describe action in the past, add **-ed**.
- To describe action in the present, add **-ing**.

❑ **Morphemes** are meaning units.
- Adding **-es** makes some nouns plural.
Example: box, boxes
- Adding **-ed** signals the past tense of a verb.
Example: lock, locked
- Adding **-ing** signals the present participle of a verb.
Example: lock, locking

WRITING ⟨ ENGLISH LANGUAGE ARTS

ACTIVITIES, ASSIGNMENTS & ASSESSMENT

❑ Composition Assignment: _____

_____

_____

Mastery Tasks   5   6   7   8   9
                     ❑   ❑   ❑   ❑   ❑

Instructional Content

WORDS TO READ/SPELL

-ix	-ap	-ax	qu-	Other
fix	yaps	Max	quick	and
mix	zaps	sax	quit	if
six			quiz	Rat Pack
				yams
				yips
				zig-zag

EXPANDED WORD LIST

lax	nix	quag	quip	quits	wax	yaks
max	quacks	quid	quips	tax	yak	zip

FIVE FAVORITE IDIOMS OR EXPRESSIONS

1. _____

2. _____

3. _____

4. _____

5. _____

Tasks for Mastery

READING

TASK 1: **Phonemic Awareness**

Student Mastery Score	Minimum Mastery Score	Maximum Mastery Score
	48	**60**
80% or more correct, progress to next Task.		

A. Listen to each word your teacher says. Write the letter that represents the first sound (phoneme) in each word you hear.

1. _____ 2. _____ 3. _____ 4. _____ 5. _____ 6. _____

7. _____ 8. _____ 9. _____ 10. _____ 11. _____ 12. _____

13. _____ 14. _____ 15. _____ 16. _____ 17. _____ 18. _____

19. _____ 20. _____ 21. _____ 22. _____ 23. _____ 24. _____

25. _____ 26. _____ 27. _____ 28. _____ 29. _____ 30. _____

Unit 7 Tasks for Mastery (continued)

B. Listen to each word your teacher says. Write the letter that represents the last sound in each word you hear.

31._____ 32._____ 33._____ 34._____ 35._____ 36._____

37._____ 38._____ 39._____ 40._____ 41._____ 42._____

43._____ 44._____ 45._____ 46._____ 47._____ 48._____

49._____ 50._____ 51._____ 52._____ 53._____ 54._____

55._____ 56._____ 57._____ 58._____ 59._____ 60._____

SPELLING

TASK 2: Sentence Dictation

Student Mastery Score	Minimum Mastery Score	Maximum Mastery Score
	16	20
80% or more correct, progress to next Task.		

Listen to the sentences your teacher says. Write the sentence that you hear. Check your spelling of new words from Unit 7. Spelling counts only for words you have already learned.

1._____

2._____

3._____

4._____

5._____

6._____

7._____

8._____

9._____

10. _____

11. _____

12. _____

13. _____

14. _____

15. _____

16. _____

17. _____

18. _____

19. _____

20. _____

Student Mastery Score	Minimum Mastery Score	Maximum Mastery Score
	17	21
80% or more correct, progress to next Task.		

TASK 3: **Spelling Word List**

Write the words that your teacher dictates on the Spelling Practice forms in the back of this book.

Student Mastery Score	Minimum Mastery Score	Maximum Mastery Score
	5	6
80% or more correct, progress to next Task.		

TASK 4: **Spelling Mastery Sentences**

1. _____

2. _____

3. _____

4. _____

5. _____

6. _____

ENGLISH/LANGUAGE ARTS

Student Mastery Score	Minimum Mastery Score	Maximum Mastery Score
	10	13
80% or more correct, progress to next Task.		

TASK 5: **Verbs**

A. Verbs are words that can describe action. Words like **jump**, **go**, **do**, and **act** are verbs. In the following, underline five words that can be used as verbs.

hid	big	Pam	ham	tack	win	ran
sick	said	in	lad	had	kick	lid

B. Verbs are words that can describe action. Verb endings can tell about the time of the action. For action in the past, add **-ed**; for action in the present, add **-ing**. Practice adding **-ing** and **-ed** endings to the following words.

kick   pack   tack

_____   _____   _____

_____   _____   _____

Student Mastery Score	Minimum Mastery Score	Maximum Mastery Score
	15	19
80% or more correct, progress to next Task.		

TASK 6: **Nouns, the Naming Words**

A noun is a word that names a person, a place, or a thing. Underline each word that can be a noun in the following list.

sack	Big B	did	big	Pam	man	ham
sick	said	in	lad	had	the	as
Nick	rack	have	to	bag	ran	has
kick	his	pig	gal	rag	fan	Sam
tack	lid	win	gas	bad	map	at

Student Mastery Score	Minimum Mastery Score	Maximum Mastery Score
	8	10
80% or more correct, progress to next Task.		

TASK 7: **Words That Can Be Nouns or Verbs**

Think about the words in the Task 5 and 6 lists. Some words might be a noun or a verb, depending on how they are used.

Example:

If you said, "Tack the picture on the wall," **tack** would be a verb, since it describes the action of the sentence.

But if you said, "The tack in my shoe made my foot hurt," **tack** would be a noun, because it would name a thing.

Find five words in the Task 5 and 6 lists that could be used as either a noun (a naming word) or a verb (an action word). Write the words on the following blanks. Explain how the words can be nouns or verbs.

1._____ 2._____ 3._____ 4._____ 5._____

6._____ 7._____ 8._____ 9._____ 10._____

Student Mastery Score	Minimum Mastery Score	Maximum Mastery Score
	10	12
80% or more correct, progress to next Task.		

TASK 8: **Concrete Nouns/Abstract Nouns**

A. Concrete nouns are words that represent something you can see and touch. Write six concrete nouns from Units 1-7 in the following blanks.

1._____ 2._____ 3._____

4._____ 5._____ 6._____

B. Abstract nouns are words that represent something you cannot see or touch, like a feeling or an idea. Write six abstract nouns from Units 1-7.

1._____   2._____   3._____

4._____   5._____   6._____

Student Mastery Score	Minimum Mastery Score	Maximum Mastery Score
	8	10
80% or more correct, progress to next Task.		

TASK 9: **Morphology**

Read each of the following sentences aloud. Then, write the correct word in the blank. Remember, add **-s** or **-es** to mean more than one (plural).

1. The (yam, yams) _____ are in this can.

2. Kim has the chips in big tin (box, boxes) _____ .

3. Sam and Al had a quick (fix, fixes) _____ for the van.

4. Pat and Tam have all the (mix, mixes) _____ to fix the dips.

5. Sis has six (cat, cats) _____ .

6. Al said the big man had some (map, maps) _____ of Atlanta.

7. Mom said, "No ifs, (and, ands), _____ or buts."

8. Did the cab have to pay (tax, taxes) _____ ?

9. Can Max fix both the (bat, bats) _____ that Al has?

10. Sit and pack (box, boxes) _____ with Nick and Sam.

Unit 8

Map

CONCEPTS & CONTENT	NOTES & EXAMPLES
READING / **SPELLING**	

READING / SPELLING

❑ Phoneme-grapheme correspondences in this unit:
Vowel sound: short /o/
The grapheme **o** represents the short vowel /o/.

❑ The vowel short /o/, spelled with **o**:
- Is the lowest on the vowel chart because the jaw is low when we say it
- Is often confused with the vowels similar in pronunciation, short /u/, /aw/.

❑ **Comprehension** questions require interpretation or translation of information. Some words signal a Comprehension question: **summarize**, **identify**, **illustrate**.

ACTIVITIES, ASSIGNMENTS & ASSESSMENT

❑ Fluency Builders   1   2   3   4

❑ Reading Assignment: *J & J Language Readers* Unit 8, Book 1: *Tam's Dog, Tab*; Book 2: *Pop Has a Nap*; Book 3: *A Pop on a Dock*

❑ Independent Reading: _____
_____
_____

Mastery Tasks   1   2   3   4   5
                     ❑   ❑   ❑   ❑   ❑

CONCEPTS & CONTENT	NOTES & EXAMPLES
❑ **Punctuation** is part of written language: **Periods** are used to signal the ends of sentences that are statements. **Question marks** are used to signal the ends of sentences that are questions. **Exclamation points** are used to signal the ends of sentences that are commands or exclamations. **Capital letters** are used: • To signal the beginnings of sentences • To signal the beginnings of names of distinct people, places, things, or ideas (proper nouns). ❑ Six Traits of Effective Writing: Focus: • Sentence Fluency • Conventions ❑ The four kinds of sentences and their punctuation marks are: • statements end with a period; • questions end with a question mark; • commands end with an exclamation point; • exclamations end with an exclamation point. ❑ Questions and their answers (statements) should share the same subject. Questions are formed with the question words: • Who (person) • What (thing) • When (time) • Where (place) • How (in what way) • Why (for what reason) ❑ Questions are also formed by putting **helping verbs** before the subject: can, did, was, were, are, etc. ❑ Proper nouns name distinct people, places, things, or ideas. Examples: Ms. West, New York, Statue of Liberty ❑ All other nouns are **common nouns**. Examples: man, store, shoe, water, school, country ❑ The Masterpiece Sentence Six-Stage Process expands sentences.	_____ _____

WRITING & ENGLISH LANGUAGE ARTS

ACTIVITIES, ASSIGNMENTS & ASSESSMENT

❑ Composition Assignment: _____
_____
_____

Mastery Tasks   6   7   8   9   10   11
                  ❑   ❑   ❑   ❑   ❑   ❑

Instructional Content

WORDS TO READ/SPELL

-ot	-ock	-om	-op	Other	Nonphonetic Words
cot	dock	Mom	pop	Bob	*taxi*
dot	lock	Tom	Pop	box	*was*
hot	rock		top	dog	
lot	sock			job	
not	tick-tock			nod	
tot					

EXPANDED WORD LIST

cob	Don	jock	mob	nog	rob	sog
cod	gob	jot	mock	pock	rod	sop
cog	got	lob	mod	pod	rot	sox
cop	hog	log	mom	pot	sob	tock
	hop	lop	mop	pox	sod	

FIVE FAVORITE IDIOMS OR EXPRESSIONS

1. _____

2. _____

3. _____

4. _____

5. _____

Tasks for Mastery

READING

Student Mastery Score	Minimum Mastery Score	Maximum Mastery Score
	48	**60**
80% or more correct, progress to next Task.		

TASK 1: **Phonemic Awareness**

A. Listen to each word your teacher says. Write the letter or letters that represent(s) the last sound in each word you hear.

1._____   2._____   3._____   4._____   5._____   6._____

7._____   8._____   9._____   10._____   11._____   12._____

13._____   14._____   15._____   16._____   17._____   18._____

19._____   20._____   21._____   22._____   23._____   24._____

25._____   26._____   27._____   28._____   29._____   30._____

B. Listen to each word your teacher says. Decide whether the vowel sound in each word you hear is a short /a/, /i/, or /o/. Write the letter <u>a</u>, <u>i</u>, or <u>o</u> to represent the phoneme you hear in each word.

31._____ 32._____ 33._____ 34._____ 35._____ 36._____

37._____ 38._____ 39._____ 40._____ 41._____ 42._____

43._____ 44._____ 45._____ 46._____ 47._____ 48._____

49._____ 50._____ 51._____ 52._____ 53._____ 54._____

55._____ 56._____ 57._____ 58._____ 59._____ 60._____

Student Mastery Score	Minimum Mastery Score	Maximum Mastery Score
	11	14
80% or more correct, progress to next Task.		

TASK 2: **Changing Spelling, Changing Words**

When one letter of a word changes, the word changes. In the following words, change a letter to create a new word. When you change the vowel, change the word. Use **<u>a</u>**, **<u>i</u>**, or **<u>o</u>**.

Example: top   tip _____   (tap would also be correct)

1. hot _____   2. sax _____

3. lick _____   4. yips _____

5. cat _____   6. Tim _____

7. lit _____   8. sick _____

9. tap _____   10. pack _____

11. dog _____   12. tock _____

13. fox _____   14. rack _____

SPELLING

Student Mastery Score	Minimum Mastery Score	Maximum Mastery Score
	16	**20**
80% or more correct, progress to next Task.		

TASK 3: **Sentence Dictation**

Listen to the sentences your teacher says. Write the sentence that you hear. Check your spelling of new words from Unit 8. Spelling counts only for words you have already learned.

1. _____

2. _____

3. _____

4. _____

5. _____

6. _____

7. _____

8. _____

9. _____

10. _____

11. _____

12. _____

13. _____

14. _____

15. _____

16. _____

17. _____

18. _____

19. _____

20. _____

Student Mastery Score	Minimum Mastery Score	Maximum Mastery Score
	17	21
80% or more correct, progress to next Task.		

TASK 4: **Spelling Word List**

Write the words that your teacher dictates on the Spelling Practice forms in the back of this book.

Student Mastery Score	Minimum Mastery Score	Maximum Mastery Score
	5	6
80% or more correct, progress to next Task.		

TASK 5: **Spelling Mastery Sentences**

1. _____

2. _____

3. _____

4. _____

5. _____

6. _____

Student Mastery Score	Minimum Mastery Score	Maximum Mastery Score
	11	14
80% or more correct, progress to next Task.		

TASK 6: **Punctuation and Capitalization**

A period (.) is used at the end of a telling sentence. A question mark (?) is used at the end of an asking sentence. Place a period or a question mark at the ends of the following two sentences.

1. Sam can bat ___   2. Can Sam bat ___

Capital letters are used at the beginning of a sentence or the beginning of a name. In the following four sentences, underline the letters that should be capitalized.

3. polly sat on a mat   4. todd can hop   5. a cab sat   6. can hank bat

These sentences may be statements or questions. Put a period (.) at the end of each statement. Put a question mark (?) at the end of each question. Underline each letter that should be a capital.

7. did dad have a long nap___

8. his dog yips and yaps___

9. at the back of the dock, a big ship was packing___

10. was the band that he went to see the rat pack___

11. did the van have to have a quick fix___

12. if nick can pack his sax in the van, can he go___

13. polly, sam, tim, and dot said they had to have a big b___

14. the pig, the dog, and the cat got sick___

ENGLISH/LANGUAGE ARTS

Student Mastery Score	Minimum Mastery Score	Maximum Mastery Score
	4	5
80% or more correct, progress to next Task.		

TASK 7: **Words and Meanings**

Use a thesaurus to find four words or phrases that mean the same thing as the following words.

1. cot _____

2. box _____

3. lot _____

4. hot _____

5. rock _____

Student Mastery Score	Minimum Mastery Score	Maximum Mastery Score
	14	18
80% or more correct, progress to next Task.		

TASK 8: **Nouns**

A. A noun is a word that names a person, place, thing, or idea. Read each of the following sentences, and underline the naming words (nouns). Study the examples and decide why each word is underlined.

Examples
1. <u>Sam</u> and his <u>dad</u> got in the <u>cab</u>. 2. The <u>job</u> of a <u>cat</u> is to nap.
3. <u>Max</u> was in the <u>back</u>. 4. <u>Sam</u> has a <u>pal</u>, <u>Dick</u>.

1. Tam sat and said, "Tab, Tab, quit it, Tab! I am mad. Max is a cat. It is bad to zap a cat."

2. Tab ran back to Tam and got on his cot.

3. Sam's pop is not at his job.

4. "The van has gas," Dad said to Sam.

5. Max can tip a big tin can.

6. The big tin can that Max zapped had bad ham in it.

B. A noun can be singular or plural. Singular means one; plural means more than one. Decide whether each of the following underlined nouns is singular or plural. Above each underlined noun, write **S** (singular) or **P** (plural).

7. Dick said, "The cats have made a mess."

8. Todd ran in to tell the kids about Mr. Hong.

9. "Can you fix the bikes, Dad?" Penny asked. "We have to go at six!"

10. The dogs at the dock were not Hank's dogs.

11. Mom got six big bags of chips and boxes of hot dogs and pop for

   the party.

12. The rock band had to have a van to get to their jobs.

C. A noun can be common or proper. A proper noun names a particular person, place, or thing. All other nouns are common nouns. Decide whether each underlined nouns below is common or proper. Above each underlined noun, write **C** (common) or **P** (proper).

13. Dick said, "The cats made a mess."

14. Todd ran in to tell the kids about Mr. Hong.

15. "Can you fix the bikes, Dad?" Polly asked. "We have to go at six!"

16. The dogs at Riverside Dock were not Hank's dogs.

17. Mrs. Hand got six big bags of chips and pop for Sam.

18. The rock band, Hot Stuff, got Todd's van to get to their jobs.

Student Mastery Score	Minimum Mastery Score	Maximum Mastery Score
	4	5
80% or more correct, progress to next Task.		

TASK 9: **Verbs**

Words that describe action are verbs. Read each of the following sentences, and underline the action words (verbs).

1. Polly hopped in the van and fastened the seat belt.

2. I locked the van when I got out.

3. Did Dad tell Hank to rock the baby?

4. His dad is not sitting at his desk.

5. The cat tips the big can and the garbage falls out.

Student Mastery Score	Minimum Mastery Score	Maximum Mastery Score
	15	19
80% or more correct, progress to next Task.		

TASK 10: **Nouns and Verbs**

A. Look at the following sentences. If the underlined word in the sentence names a person, place, thing, or idea, write **N** (noun). If the following underlined word describes action, write **V** (verb).

1. Tab had Tam's <u>sock</u>. _____

2. Max <u>rocks</u> the tin can. _____

3. In the van, Sam <u>nods</u> at Tom. _____

4. I had the <u>box</u> with a lock on it. _____

5. The kids can pass the <u>quiz</u>. _____

6. <u>Pass</u> the ham and the yams. _____

7. On the last <u>pass</u>, Sam got the ball and ran to win. _____

8. <u>Honk</u> at the van on the dock. _____

9. Did Sid's model ship <u>sink</u> in the pond? _____

10. The <u>sock</u> Tam lost was pink. _____

11. Bill got his <u>gang</u> to sing the song with the rock band. _____

12. Did Dad <u>quiz</u> Sid and Sam? _____

13. <u>Pop</u> can fix it at his job. _____

14. He got a new <u>lock</u> on his back door. _____

15. <u>Lock</u> the back door. _____

B. Some words can be used as either nouns or verbs. In the sentences you just read, what words were used as both a noun and a verb? Explain why.

_____

Student Mastery Score	Minimum Mastery Score	Maximum Mastery Score
	8	10
80% or more correct, progress to next Task.		

TASK 11: **Choosing the Suffix**

We will read each of the following sentences aloud. Think about the suffix needed, then write the correct word in the blank. Remember:

Add **-s** or **-es** to mean more than one (plural).
Add **-ing** to mean present time.
Add **-ed** to mean past time.

1. The man has (locked, locking) _____ his cab.

2. Tam and Pat are (zipped, zipping) _____ the bags.

3. Max is (napped, napping) _____ with Dad.

4. Al is (logged, logging) _____ on to his PC.

5. Kim (topped, topping) _____ the bun with jam.

6. Check the (top, tops) _____ of the cans of pop.

7. The top (cop, cops) _____ got the robbers.

8. Sam said, "Is there a (tax, taxes) _____ on the socks?"

9. The tick- (tock, tocks) _____ of the clocks got mom mad.

10. Six (kid, kids) _____ were in a cab.

Unit 9

Map

CONCEPTS & CONTENT	NOTES & EXAMPLES

READING

SPELLING

❑ The graphemes representing /f/, /l/, /s/, and /z/ are usually doubled at the end of one-syllable words.

❑ The double **f**, **l**, **s**, **z** rule:

Words ending with /f/, /l/, /s/, or /z/ after a short vowel almost always double the final consonant.

❑ The 1-1-1 doubling rule:

When a word ending (suffix) begins with a vowel and is added to a
  1 syllable word with
  1 final consonant preceded by
  1 vowel

double the final consonant. Example: **sit** + **ing** = sitting

---

ACTIVITIES, ASSIGNMENTS & ASSESSMENT

❑ Fluency Builders   1   2   3   4

❑ Reading Assignment: *J & J Language Readers* Unit 9, Book 1: *Miss Pitt*; Book 2: *Bill and Jill*; Book 3: *Will Al Win?*

❑ Independent Reading: _____

_____

_____

Mastery Tasks   1   2   3   4   5
                     ❑   ❑   ❑   ❑   ❑

CONCEPTS & CONTENT	NOTES & EXAMPLES

❑ Some words are capitalized depending upon usage.
Example: When **Miss** is part of a proper noun (**Miss Pitt**) as contrasted with **miss** as a common noun (a hit or miss trial) or a verb (I miss you).

❑ Six Traits of Effective Writing:
Focus:

• Sentence Fluency

• Conventions

❑ Masterpiece Sentence
Focus: Stage 1: Prepare Your Canvas

A sentence has a subject and a **predicate**.

❑ Some words have many different meanings and different possible functions. Examples: These words can be nouns or verbs: **pin**, **lock**, **miss**. Their meaning and function are determined by the context in which they are used.

WRITING ‹ ENGLISH LANGUAGE ARTS

ACTIVITIES, ASSIGNMENTS & ASSESSMENT

❑ Composition Assignment: _____
_____
_____

Mastery Tasks   6   7   8   9   10   11   12
                        ❑   ❑   ❑   ❑   ❑   ❑   ❑

Instructional Content

WORDS TO READ/SPELL

-ill	-iss	-ass	Other	Nonphonetic Word
Bill	hiss	lass	doll	*you*
hill	kiss	pass	jazz	
Jill	miss		Liz	
pill	Miss		off	
quill			Pitt	
sill			toss	
till				
will				

EXPANDED WORD LIST

bass	dill	gill	loll	mill	moss	tiff
bill	fill	Hill	loss	Miss	rill	toss
boss	gaff	kill	miff	moll	Ross	Will

FIVE FAVORITE IDIOMS OR EXPRESSIONS

1. _____

2. _____

3. _____

4. _____

5. _____

Tasks for Mastery

READING

Student Mastery Score	Minimum Mastery Score	Maximum Mastery Score
	48	60
80% or more correct, progress to next Task.		

TASK 1: **Phonemic Awareness**

A. Listen to each word your teacher says. Write the letter or letters that represent the last sound you hear in each word.

1. _____   2. _____   3. _____   4. _____   5. _____   6. _____

7. _____   8. _____   9. _____   10. _____   11. _____   12. _____

13. _____   14. _____   15. _____   16. _____   17. _____   18. _____

19. _____   20. _____   21. _____   22. _____   23. _____   24. _____

25. _____   26. _____   27. _____   28. _____   29. _____   30. _____

B. Listen to each word your teacher says. Decide whether the vowel sound in each word you hear is /a/, /i/, or /o/. Write the letter **a**, **i**, or **o** to show which sound you hear in each word.

31._____ 32._____ 33._____ 34._____ 35._____ 36._____

37._____ 38._____ 39._____ 40._____ 41._____ 42._____

43._____ 44._____ 45._____ 46._____ 47._____ 48._____

49._____ 50._____ 51._____ 52._____ 53._____ 54._____

55._____ 56._____ 57._____ 58._____ 59._____ 60._____

SPELLING

TASK 2: **Sentence Dictation**

Student Mastery Score	Minimum Mastery Score	Maximum Mastery Score
	16	**20**
80% or more correct, progress to next Task.		

Listen to the sentences your teacher says. Write the sentence that you hear. Check your spelling of new words from Unit 9. Spelling counts only for words you have already learned. (*Note: As punctuation and capitalization rules were taught in Unit 8, you are now responsible for what has been directly taught.*)

1._____

2._____

3._____

4._____

5._____

6._____

7._____

8._____

9._____

10. _____

11. _____

12. _____

13. _____

14. _____

15. _____

16. _____

17. _____

18. _____

19. _____

20. _____

Student Mastery Score	Minimum Mastery Score	Maximum Mastery Score
	45	56
80% or more correct, progress to next Task.		

TASK 3: **Spelling Review**

A. Your teacher will say a word in a sentence. Then your teacher will repeat the word alone. Spell each word your teacher says.

1. _____ 2. _____ 3. _____ 4. _____ 5. _____ 6. _____

7. _____ 8. _____ 9. _____ 10. _____ 11. _____ 12. _____

13. _____ 14. _____ 15. _____ 16. _____ 17. _____ 18. _____

19. _____ 20. _____ 21. _____ 22. _____ 23. _____ 24. _____

25. _____ 26. _____ 27. _____ 28. _____ 29. _____ 30. _____

31. _____ 32. _____ 33. _____ 34. _____ 35. _____ 36. _____

37. _____ 38. _____ 39. _____ 40. _____ 41. _____ 42. _____

43. _____ 44. _____ 45. _____ 46. _____ 47. _____ 48. _____

B. Go back and circle the words that you missed so that you can practice them.

C. In the following blanks, write the words that are hardest for you to remember.

49. _____ 50. _____ 51. _____ 52. _____

53. _____ 54. _____ 55. _____ 56. _____

Student Mastery Score	Minimum Mastery Score	Maximum Mastery Score
	16	20
80% or more correct, progress to next Task.		

TASK 4: **Spelling Word List**

Write the words that your teacher dictates on the Spelling Practice forms in the back of this book.

Student Mastery Score	Minimum Mastery Score	Maximum Mastery Score
	6	7
80% or more correct, progress to next Task.		

TASK 5: **Spelling Mastery Sentences**

1. _____

2. _____

3. _____

4. _____

5. _____

6. _____

7. _____

WRITING

Student Mastery Score	Minimum Mastery Score	Maximum Mastery Score
	12	**15**
80% or more correct, progress to next Task.		

TASK 6: **Punctuation**

Punctuation is the mechanical part of written language:

Periods are used at the ends of sentences that are statements.

Question marks are used at the ends of sentences that are questions.

Capital letters are used at the beginnings of sentences and at the beginnings of names of particular people, places, or things (proper nouns).

Cut an article from a newspaper or magazine. Find five periods, five question marks, and five capital letters. Explain why each of these punctuation marks is used in the article.

ENGLISH/LANGUAGE ARTS

Student Mastery Score	Minimum Mastery Score	Maximum Mastery Score
	38	48
80% or more correct, progress to next Task.		

TASK 7: **Nouns and Verbs**

A word that describes action is a verb. Read the following four examples. Decide why each circled word is a verb.

Examples:
1. (Pass) the hot dogs to me. 2. Bill can (lock) his van.
3. Tim (ran) to Miss Goff's van. 4. Pam will (fix) a can of pop.

A. In the following sentences, circle each action word.

 1. "Pin this on your cap, Tim," said Miss Hill.

 2. Dick passed the cans of pop.

 3. Jill's mom and dad will rock the baby.

 4. Rick said, "I will zap Miss Pitt's quiz."

 5. "Toss the cap to him," Mick said.

 6. Bill boxed Tim.

 7. You kissed the doll I got for Polly.

 8. Kim, Tam, Sid, and Sam mixed the pop and ice cream.

 9. Al rips the kit.

10. The kids will lock the van.

B. A word that names a person, place, thing, or idea is a noun. In the ten sentences that you have just read, underline each word that names a person, place, thing, or idea.

C. Nouns that name a particular person, place, thing, or idea are proper nouns. In the following blanks, write eight proper nouns from the sentences presented in B.

_____   _____   _____   _____

_____   _____   _____   _____

D. Practice adding **-ed** and **-ing** to the following action verbs. When the sound pattern is consonant-vowel-consonant (**cvc**), as in **rip** and **bat**, double the last consonant before adding **-ed** or **-ing**.

	add **-ed**	add **-ing**
rip	_____	_____
kiss	_____	_____
bat	_____	_____
mix	_____	_____
lock	_____	_____
toss	_____	_____

Student Mastery Score	Minimum Mastery Score	Maximum Mastery Score
	4	5
80% or more correct, progress to next Task.		

TASK 8: **Words and Meanings**

Use a thesaurus to find four words that mean the same thing as the following words.

1. lass _____

2. doll _____

3. pass _____

4. will _____

5. kiss _____

Student Mastery Score	Minimum Mastery Score	Maximum Mastery Score
	17	21
80% or more correct, progress to next Task.		

TASK 9: **Thinking About Words**

A. Think of words that refer to things in a home. List five words in each category.

Living Room	Bedroom	Kitchen
_____	_____	_____
_____	_____	_____
_____	_____	_____
_____	_____	_____
_____	_____	_____

B. Words that describe action are verbs. List two verbs that you can associate with each of these same categories.

Living Room	Bedroom	Kitchen
_____	_____	_____
_____	_____	_____

Student Mastery Score	Minimum Mastery Score	Maximum Mastery Score
	12	15
80% or more correct, progress to next Task.		

TASK 10: **Sentences**

A. A sentence is a group of words that has a complete idea. Sentences may be questions (asking sentences) or statements (telling sentences). Use the phrases here to make a sentence that either asks a question or makes a statement, as specified. You will only be responsible for spelling correctly the words you have learned.

Examples:

(question) had his hat   Can you nab his hat?

(statement) in his bag   Mac had a map in his bag.

(question) tag the rim   _____

(statement) ribbed the sack   _____

(question) in the van   _____

(statement) missed the taxi   _____

(question) if his job was bad   _____

(statement) passed the sax   _____

(question) fit in the box   _____

(statement) had a bad back   _____

(question) a pop quiz   _____

(statement) sat at the dock   _____

B. Rewrite the sentences that asked a question from the previous activity to make them statements.

Example: Can you nab his hat?   (statement) You can nab his hat.

1. _____

2. _____

3. _____

4. _____

5. _____

Student Mastery Score	Minimum Mastery Score	Maximum Mastery Score
	8	10
80% or more correct, progress to next Task.		

TASK 11: **Reviewing Subjects in Sentences**

The subject names a person, place, thing, or idea that the sentence tells about. Circle the subjects in the sentences you wrote for Task 10.

Student Mastery Score	Minimum Mastery Score	Maximum Mastery Score
	8	10
80% or more correct, progress to next Task.		

TASK 12: **Choosing the Suffix**

We will read each of the following sentences aloud. Think about the correct suffix needed, then write the correct word in the blank. Remember:

Add **-s** or **-es** to mean more than one (plural).

Add **-ing** to mean present time.

Add **-ed** to mean past time.

1. The Cats had six (loss, losses) _____ but got the last win.

2. I have had six (quizzed, quizzes) _____ .

3. Mom has hot (yam, yams) _____ in the big pot.

4. Dad (tossing, tossed) _____ a log on the fire.

5. The pods that we are (popped, popping) _____ are big pods.

6. Ross (tossed, tossing) _____ the mop on the deck.

7. Miss Hill said, "I am (nodded, nodding) _____ if you have got it on the quiz."

8. Tom is (filled, filling) _____ the van with gas.

9. The (gills, gilled) _____ of the fish are big.

10. The man that (robbed, robbing) _____ the bank is locked in the van.

Unit 10

Map

CONCEPTS & CONTENT	NOTES & EXAMPLES

READING

❑ The letters **ng** represent one sound, /ng/. This sound is found only after the vowel in a syllable.
The letters **nk** represent two sounds, /ng/ and /k/.

❑ No English words begin with **-ng** or **-nk**.

❑ **Application** questions require the use of information. Some words signal an Application question: **generalize**, **infer**, **apply**.

❑ Stories have different parts. The **response** to the initiating event in a story describes how the characters react to the initiating event or problem.

SPELLING ⎰

_____
_____
_____
_____
_____
_____
_____
_____
_____
_____
_____
_____
_____
_____
_____
_____
_____
_____
_____
_____
_____
_____

ACTIVITIES, ASSIGNMENTS & ASSESSMENT

❑ Fluency Builders   1   2   3   4

❑ Reading Assignment: *J & J Language Readers* Unit 10, Book 1: *Bang, Ring, Sing!*; Book 2: *The King of the Rink*; Book 3: *Bang the Gong*

❑ Independent Reading: _____
_____
_____

Mastery Tasks   1   2   3   4
                     ❑   ❑   ❑   ❑

CONCEPTS & CONTENT	NOTES & EXAMPLES	

❑ Six Traits of Effective Writing:
Focus:

- Sentence Fluency

- Conventions

   Statements can be transformed into questions, and questions into statements.

❑ Masterpiece Sentence
Focus: Stage 2: Paint Your Predicate

   The predicate can be expanded through the questions **where**, **when**, **how**.

WRITING ∼ ENGLISH LANGUAGE ARTS

ACTIVITIES, ASSIGNMENTS & ASSESSMENT

❑ Composition Assignment: _____

_____

_____

Mastery Tasks   5   6   7   8   9   10   11   12
                     ❑   ❑   ❑   ❑   ❑   ❑   ❑   ❑

Instructional Content

WORDS TO READ/SPELL

-ang	-ing	-ong	-onk	-ink	-ank	Nonphonetic Word
bang	king	ding-dong	honk	pink	rank	*what*
gang	ring	gong		rink	yank	
sang	sing	long		sink		
	wings	song				

EXPANDED WORD LIST

conk	fink	King	ling	pang	tong	Yank
dank	hang	kink	link	sank	wink	zing
fang	Hank	lank	mink	tang	yang	

FIVE FAVORITE IDIOMS OR EXPRESSIONS

1. _____

2. _____

3. _____

4. _____

5. _____

Tasks for Mastery

READING

Student Mastery Score	Minimum Mastery Score	Maximum Mastery Score
	43	54
80% or more correct, progress to next Task.		

TASK 1: **Phonemic Awareness**

A. Listen to each word your teacher says. Write the letters that represent the sound or sounds you hear after the vowel sound in each word: **-ng** or **-nk**.

1. _____   2. _____   3. _____   4. _____   5. _____   6. _____

7. _____   8. _____   9. _____   10. _____   11. _____   12. _____

13. _____   14. _____   15. _____   16. _____   17. _____   18. _____

B. Listen to each word your teacher says. Decide whether the vowel sound in each word you hear is /a/, /i/, or /o/. Write **a**, **i**, or **o** to represent the vowel sound you hear in each word.

19. _____   20. _____   21. _____   22. _____   23. _____   24. _____

25. _____   26. _____   27. _____   28. _____   29. _____   30. _____

31. _____   32. _____   33. _____   34. _____   35. _____   36. _____

C. Listen to each word your teacher says. After you hear the word, write the letter that represents the word's first sound.

37._____ 38._____ 39._____ 40._____ 41._____ 42._____

43._____ 44._____ 45._____ 46._____ 47._____ 48._____

49._____ 50._____ 51._____ 52._____ 53._____ 54._____

SPELLING

Student Mastery Score	Minimum Mastery Score	Maximum Mastery Score
	16	20
80% or more correct, progress to next Task.		

TASK 2: **Sentence Dictation**

Listen to the sentences your teacher says. Write the sentence that you hear. Check your spelling of new words from Unit 10. Spelling counts only for words that you have already learned.

1._____

2._____

3._____

4._____

5._____

6._____

7._____

8._____

9._____

10._____

11._____

12. _____

13. _____

14. _____

15. _____

16. _____

17. _____

18. _____

19. _____

20. _____

Student Mastery Score	Minimum Mastery Score	Maximum Mastery Score
	17	21
80% or more correct, progress to next Task.		

TASK 3: **Spelling Word List**

Write the words that your teacher dictates on the Spelling Practice forms in the back of this book.

Student Mastery Score	Minimum Mastery Score	Maximum Mastery Score
	4	5
80% or more correct, progress to next Task.		

TASK 4: **Spelling Mastery Sentences**

1. _____

2. _____

3. _____

4. _____

5. _____

ENGLISH/LANGUAGE ARTS

Student Mastery Score	Minimum Mastery Score	Maximum Mastery Score
	8	10
80% or more correct, progress to next Task.		

TASK 5: **Sentences**

A sentence is a group of words that has a complete thought or idea.
   These words are a sentence: Tim got the socks when he was at the mall.
   These words are not a sentence: got the socks when he was at the mall

The second example tells what happened, but not who performed the action (subject of sentence). It does not have complete meaning.

Read each of the following groups of words. If the words are a complete sentence put an **S** in the blank. If the words are not a complete sentence put an **X** in the blank.

_____   1. what the king of the land sings

_____   2. if they went to sing with the king

_____   3. she sat on the sill and had a can of pop

_____   4. he did not wink at Pam; Pam winked at him

_____   5. what he did for her mom and dad

_____   6. Bill said that his mom was sick

_____   7. the gong will ring if I win the game

_____   8. the dog that was at the dock

_____   9. a big box of hot dogs and pop in the van

_____   10. the kids that were at the skating rink

Student Mastery Score	Minimum Mastery Score	Maximum Mastery Score
	10	12
80% or more correct, progress to next Task.		

TASK 6: **Words and Meanings**

Use a thesaurus to find three words or phrases that mean the same thing as the following words.

1. tank _____

2. ring _____

3. gang _____

4. sing _____

Student Mastery Score	Minimum Mastery Score	Maximum Mastery Score
	16	20
80% or more correct, progress to next Task.		

TASK 7: **Complete Sentences Have Subjects and Predicates**

A sentence is a group of words that has a complete thought or idea. A sentence must have a subject. The subject names the person, place, thing, or idea that the sentence describes. The underlined words in Example 1 are subjects.

Example 1:

Tim got the socks at the mall.

The man that sang was the winner.

The song that the man sang was long.

The rink had a ring toss last night.

A sentence must have a predicate. The predicate describes the action of the subject. The underlined words in Example 2 are predicates.

Example 2:

Tim got the socks at the mall.

The kid that sang won the prize.

The man boxed in the ring.

The gang sang last night.

A. Read each of the following sentences. Circle the subject of each sentence. Underline the predicate of each sentence.

1. The king of the land sings.

2. They sang with the king.

3. She honked at her dad.

4. He winked at Pam.

5. Her mom kissed dad.

6. Bill said that his mom was sick.

7. The gong will ring if I win the game.

8. The dog yapped at the dock.

9. I fixed hot dogs and pop for Pam.

10. The kids skated at the rink.

B. Study each of the sentences you have just read. Note that each sentence is a statement. Change each statement to a question. Be sure to use a question mark at the end. Two have already been completed for you.

11. Does the king of the land sing? _____

12. _____

13. _____

14. _____

15. _____

16. Did Bill say that his mom was sick? _____

17. _____

18. _____

19. _____

20. _____

Student Mastery Score	Minimum Mastery Score	Maximum Mastery Score
	8	10
80% or more correct, progress to next Task.		

TASK 8: **Choosing the Suffix**

We will read each of the following sentences aloud. Think about the suffix. then write the correct word in the blank. Remember:

    Add **-s** or **-es** to mean more than one (plural).

    Add **-ing** to mean present time.

    Add **-ed** to mean past time.

1. Tom (winked, winking) _____ at Kim.

2. Sis had the (rods, rodding) _____ at the dock.

3. I will pick up these (tong, tongs) _____ on the grill.

4. Pat (zinged, zinging) _____ a toss to Sam.

5. Dad had felt hot (panged, pangs) _____ in his back.

6. Hank Ross is (batted, batting) _____ last.

7. Dr. King was (killed, killing) _____ in 1967.

8. The cabs and vans (honking, honked) _____ in the hot sun.

9. The kids sang a song to the (Yanks, Yanked) _____ when they won.

10. The big man (banged, banging) _____ the gong at the end.

Unit 11

Map

CONCEPTS & CONTENT	NOTES & EXAMPLES

READING

SPELLING ~

❑ A **digraph** is a two-letter combination that spells one unique sound. The consonant digraphs are:

- **th** stands for both a voiced /*th*/ (this, that, them) and voiceless /*th*/ (thin, thick, math) phoneme.

- **wh** is the voiceless equivalent of /*w*/.

- **ch** is the voiceless equivalent of /*j*/.

- **sh** is a continuous hissy sound (fricative) that contrasts with /*zh*/ as in vision, its voiced equivalent.

❑ Application questions require the use of information. Some words signal an application question: **predict**, **use**, **show**.

ACTIVITIES, ASSIGNMENTS & ASSESSMENT

❑ Fluency Builders   1   2   3   4

❑ Reading Assignment: *J & J Language Readers* Unit 11, Book 1: *Al's Wish*; Book 2: *Thin Thad*; Book 3: *Chick's Fish Shack*

❑ Independent Reading: _____
_____
_____

Mastery Tasks   1   2   3   4   5
                     ❑   ❑   ❑   ❑   ❑

CONCEPTS & CONTENT	NOTES & EXAMPLES

❑ Six Traits of Effective Writing:
Focus: Sentence Fluency
 	
❑ Masterpiece Sentence
Focus:
    Stage 2: Paint Your Predicate
    Stage 3: Move the Predicate Painters	

WRITING ι ENGLISH LANGUAGE ARTS

ACTIVITIES, ASSIGNMENTS & ASSESSMENT

❑ Composition Assignment: _____

_____

_____

Mastery Tasks   6   7   8   9   10   11   12
                   ❑   ❑   ❑   ❑   ❑   ❑   ❑

Instructional Content

WORDS TO READ/SPELL

sh		th		ch	wh	Nonphonetic Words
cash	ships	bath	thin	chap	wham	*are*
dash	shock	math	thing	chat	which	*put*
dish	shop	than	think	chill	whiff	
fish	shot	thank	this	chip		
shack	wish	that	with	pinch		
shall		thick		rich		
				which		

EXPANDED WORD LIST

bash	chips	gosh	posh	sham	shocks	whiffs	whop
baths	chit	hash	pith	shams	shod	Whig	whops
Chad	chits	inch	ranch	shank	shops	whim	
chats	chock	josh	rash	shanks	shots	whims	
chicks	chocks	lash	Roth	shim	thong	winch	
chills	chop	mash	sash	shims	thongs	whip	
chin	chops	moth	shad	shin	whack	whips	
chink	finch	moths	shag	shins	whacks	whit	
chins	gash	paths	shags	ship	whams	whiz	

FIVE FAVORITE IDIOMS OR EXPRESSIONS

1. _____

2. _____

3. _____

4. _____

5. _____

Tasks for Mastery

READING

Student Mastery Score	Minimum Mastery Score	Maximum Mastery Score
	43	**54**
80% or more correct, progress to next Task.		

TASK 1: **Phonemic Awareness**

A. Listen to each word your teacher says. Write the letter(s) that represents the sound you hear after the vowel in each word. Some of the sounds will be represented by digraphs (two letters that represent one consonant sound).

1._____   2._____   3._____   4._____   5._____   6._____

7._____   8._____   9._____   10._____   11._____   12._____

13._____   14._____   15._____   16._____   17._____   18._____

B. Listen to each word your teacher says. Decide whether the vowel sound in each word you hear is /a/, /i/, or /o/. Write **a**, **i**, or **o** to represent the vowel sound you hear.

19._____   20._____   21._____   22._____   23._____   24._____

25._____   26._____   27._____   28._____   29._____   30._____

31._____   32._____   33._____   34._____   35._____   36._____

C. Listen to each word your teacher says. Write the letter(s) that represents the first sound you hear in each word. Some of the sounds will be represented by digraphs (two letters that represent one consonant sound).

37. _____ 38. _____ 39. _____ 40. _____ 41. _____ 42. _____

43. _____ 44. _____ 45. _____ 46. _____ 47. _____ 48. _____

49. _____ 50. _____ 51. _____ 52. _____ 53. _____ 54. _____

Student Mastery Score	Minimum Mastery Score	Maximum Mastery Score
	3	3
80% or more correct, progress to next Task.		

TASK 2: **Nonphonetic Words**

This unit's nonphonetic words are **put** and **are**. How would they sound if they were phonetically regular? What happens to the sound of <u>u</u> when <u>-ing</u>, <u>-s</u>, or <u>-er</u> endings are added to **put**? When **putting** is spoken of in golf, how does the <u>u</u> sound?

put + ing _____   put + s _____   put + er _____

SPELLING

Student Mastery Score	Minimum Mastery Score	Maximum Mastery Score
	26	32
80% or more correct, progress to next Task.		

TASK 3: **Letter Pairs**

Unit 11 has words with <u>sh</u>, <u>th</u>, <u>ch</u>, and <u>wh</u> digraphs. Write the words in the following columns. As you write the letter pairs (digraphs), say aloud the sounds they represent.

sh   **th**   **ch**   **wh**

_____   _____   _____   _____

_____   _____   _____   _____

_____   _____   _____   _____

_____   _____   _____

_____   _____   _____

_____   _____   _____

_____   _____   _____

_____   _____

_____   _____

_____   _____

Student Mastery Score	Minimum Mastery Score	Maximum Mastery Score
	17	21
80% or more correct, progress to next Task.		

TASK 4: **Spelling Word List**

Write the words that your teacher dictates on the Spelling Practice forms in the back of this book.

Student Mastery Score	Minimum Mastery Score	Maximum Mastery Score
	5	6
80% or more correct, progress to next Task.		

TASK 5: **Spelling Mastery Sentences**

1. _____

2. _____

3. _____

4. _____

5. _____

6. _____

ENGLISH/LANGUAGE ARTS

Student Mastery Score	Minimum Mastery Score	Maximum Mastery Score
	3	4
80% or more correct, progress to next Task.		

TASK 6: **Definitions**

The word **chap** has many meanings. Use a thesaurus to find four words that mean the same thing as **chap**.

_____   _____   _____   _____

Student Mastery Score	Minimum Mastery Score	Maximum Mastery Score
	7	9
80% or more correct, progress to next Task.		

TASK 7: **Word Forms**

Think about the following words. Are these words nouns (names of persons, places, or things)? Are they verbs (action words)? Some words can be both. Write **N** (noun), **V** (verb), or **N+V** beside each word.

1. chip _____   2. wish _____   3. thank _____

4. chill _____   5. thing _____   6. call _____

7. wham _____   8. dish _____   9. fish _____

Student Mastery Score	Minimum Mastery Score	Maximum Mastery Score
	8	10
80% or more correct, progress to next Task.		

TASK 8: **Pronouncing and Writing Words**

A. Read each of the following sentence pairs. Remember, an **-ed** ending means past time. Be sure to pronounce **-s** and **-ed** endings clearly. (**-ed** sometimes sounds like /t/.)

1. He shocks his teacher. He shocked his teacher.
2. Do not chip the glass. The glass is chipped.
3. I will chill the pops. We chilled the pops.
4. Put in a pinch of salt. We pinched the bread.
5. The shops are at the dock. We shopped at the dock.
6. She dashed off after work. Do not dash off.
7. Thad shipped the package. Thad will ship the package.
8. I got a whiff of the stuff. I whiffed the stuff.
9. Did you cash the check? I cashed my check.
10. Chick will dish up the food. Chick dished up the food.

B. Listen to the sentences your teacher says. Write the ending of the word that your teacher repeats. Be careful to use the letters that represent the ending you hear: **-s** or **-ed**.

1. _____

2. _____

3. _____

4. _____

5. _____

6. _____

7. _____

8. _____

9. _____

10. _____

TASK 9: **Words Used as Nouns and Verbs, and as Subjects and Predicates**

Student Mastery Score	Minimum Mastery Score	Maximum Mastery Score
	24	30
80% or more correct, progress to next Task.		

A. Some words can be nouns or verbs. Read the following sentences and place an **X** in the appropriate blank to indicate whether the underlined word is a noun or a verb.

	Noun	Verb
1. He <u>chipped</u> the lid off of the chilled jam.		
2. The <u>ship</u> was tossed back to the dock.		
3. We jammed on a sax at the jazz <u>shop</u>.		
4. I <u>wish</u> that I did not have to quit math.		
5. The <u>chip</u> in the dish was big.		
6. Can you <u>ring</u> the gong?		
7. The box had a jammed <u>lock</u>.		
8. His sack was <u>packed</u> with fish and chips.		
9. He <u>bagged</u> the ham in a pink sack.		
10. He had a big <u>rock</u>.		

B. Some words can be used as subjects and predicates. In the preceding sentences, circle the subject (a noun that the sentence tells about) and draw a square around the predicate (a verb or verb phrase that tells what the subject does or is).

TASK 10: **Reviewing Nouns, Verbs, Subjects, and Predicates**

Student Mastery Score	Minimum Mastery Score	Maximum Mastery Score
	24	30
80% or more correct, progress to next Task.		

Refer to the sentences in the previous task. Rewrite each one using the underlined noun as a verb or the underlined verb as a noun. Remember, you may use different verb endings that describe time of the action (**-ed**, and **-ing**) to complete the sentence. You may use any words and will only be responsible for correctly spelling those you have been taught.

Example: We were chatting in the <u>shop</u>.
             We <u>shopped</u> with his mom and dad.

1. _____

2. _____

3. _____

4. _____

5. _____

6. _____

7. _____

8. _____

9. _____

10. _____

B. Circle the subject and draw a square around the predicate.

Student Mastery Score	Minimum Mastery Score	Maximum Mastery Score
	3	3
80% or more correct, progress to next Task.		

TASK 11: **Word Origins**

Read this sentence: "The kids think Miss Hill is rad."

A. What does **rad** mean?

_____

B. When **rad** was first used in this way, it was the first syllable of the word **radical**. Look up the word **radical** in the dictionary. What does **radical** mean?

_____

C. What is the origin of the word **radical**?

_____

Student Mastery Score	Minimum Mastery Score	Maximum Mastery Score
	8	10
80% or more correct, progress to next Task.		

TASK 12: **Morphology**

We will read each of the following sentences aloud. Think about the correct suffix. Then, write the correct word in the blank. Remember:

Add **-s** or **-es** to mean more than one (plural).

Add **-ing** to mean present time.

Add **-ed** to mean past time.

1. Max has an inch-long (gash, gashes) _____ on his chin.

2. Tam (shopped, shopping) _____ for CDs at the mall.

3. Dad (mashes, mashing) _____ potatoes.

4. The tablet (fizz, fizzes) _____ when you drop it in the glass.

5. Mr. Ross said that the men (wished, wishes) _____ for lots of things.

6. The man (shipped, shipping) _____ lots of his pigs to Wisconsin.

7. Miss Whisk said, "Are you (thinking, thinks) _____ of the math quiz"?

8. Tom's cat is (shedding, shedded) _____ .

9. Chad fed the (kid, kids) _____ that got to the shop at ten.

10. Peg is (ringing, rings) _____ the bells for the class.

Unit 12

Map

CONCEPTS & CONTENT	NOTES & EXAMPLES
❑ Phoneme-grapheme correspondence in this unit: Vowel sound: short /e/ The letter **e** represents the short /e/ vowel sound.	_____

READING

SPELLING

ACTIVITIES, ASSIGNMENTS & ASSESSMENT

❑ Fluency Builders 1 2 3 4 Review

❑ Reading Assignment: _J & J Language Readers_ Unit 12, Book 1: _Jen Well's Pet Shop_; Book 2: _Ted's Shell Shop_; Book 3: _Ken Bell_

❑ Independent Reading: _____
_____
_____

Mastery Tasks   1   2   3   4   5   6   7
                  ❑   ❑   ❑   ❑   ❑   ❑   ❑

CONCEPTS & CONTENT	NOTES & EXAMPLES

❑ Use the **apostrophe** + <u>s</u> (' + <u>s</u>) to show ownership (possession) of a noun. Example: cat's = belongs to the cat

❑ Six Traits of Effective Writing:
Focus:
  • Ideas
  • Organization
  • Voice
  • Word Choice
  • Sentence Fluency
  • Conventions

❑ Masterpiece Sentence
Focus: Stage 2: Paint Your Predicate

WRITING ~ ENGLISH LANGUAGE ARTS

ACTIVITIES, ASSIGNMENTS & ASSESSMENT

❑ Composition Assignment: _____

_____

_____

Mastery Tasks   8   9   10   11   12   13
                 ❑   ❑   ❑   ❑   ❑   ❑

Instructional Content

WORDS TO READ/SPELL

-ed	-eg	-ell	-et	-en	-ess	Other	Nonphonetic Words
bed	beg	bell	bet	Jen	chess	them	*could*
led	leg	Bell	get	Ken	less	yes	*should*
red		fell	let	men	mess		*would*
Ted		Nell	met	pen			
		sell	nets	ten			
		shell	pet	then			
		tell	set	when			
		well	vet				
		Wells	wet				
		yell	yet				

EXPANDED WORD LIST

beck	check	fed	hen	jets	mesh	pegs	sells	vex	whet
beds	checks	fez	hens	keg	neck	pens	sets	web	yells
begs	deck	gets	hex	kegs	necks	pep	shed	webs	yen
bells	decks	heck	Jeff	legs	pecks	pets	sheds	wed	
Beth	dell	hem	jell	lens	Peg	reps	tells	wen	
bets	dens	hems	jells	lets	peg	revs	tens	wets	

FIVE FAVORITE IDIOMS OR EXPRESSIONS

1. _____

2. _____

3. _____

4. _____

5. _____

~~~~~~

Tasks for Mastery

READING

Student Mastery Score	Minimum Mastery Score	Maximum Mastery Score
	48	60
80% or more correct, progress to next Task.		

TASK 1: Phonemic Awareness

A. Listen to each word your teacher says. Decide whether the vowel sound in each word you hear is /a/, /e/, /i/, or /o/. Write **a**, **e**, **i**, or **o** in each of the following blanks to represent the vowel sound (phoneme) you hear.

1._____   2._____   3._____   4._____   5._____   6._____

7._____   8._____   9._____   10._____   11._____   12._____

13._____   14._____   15._____   16._____   17._____   18._____

19._____   20._____   21._____   22._____   23._____   24._____

25._____   26._____   27._____   28._____   29._____   30._____

B. Listen to each word your teacher says. Write the letter that represents the last sound (phoneme) in each word you hear. Some of the sounds may be represented by digraphs (you will need two letters to represent one last sound).

31. ___	32. ___	33. ___	34. ___	35. ___	36. ___
37. ___	38. ___	39. ___	40. ___	41. ___	42. ___
43. ___	44. ___	45. ___	46. ___	47. ___	48. ___
49. ___	50. ___	51. ___	52. ___	53. ___	54. ___
55. ___	56. ___	57. ___	58. ___	59. ___	60. ___

Student Mastery Score	Minimum Mastery Score	Maximum Mastery Score
	4	5
80% or more correct, progress to next Task.		

TASK 2: **Identifying Signal Words**

Read each question. Decide whether the question is a Knowledge, Comprehension, or Application question. Put an **X** in the box marked **K** if it is a Knowledge question. Put an **X** in the box marked **C** if it is a Comprehension question. Put an **X** in the box marked **A** if the question is an Application question. Underline the signal words.

K	C	A	
			1. What was Mat planning?
			2. Predict who will win.
			3. List the questions you would ask a race car driver.
			4. There is a crash at Zig Zag pass. Imagine what happened and tell about it.
			5. Decide if the statement is true or false. Explain.

Student Mastery Score	Minimum Mastery Score	Maximum Mastery Score
	4	5
80% or more correct, progress to next Task.		

TASK 3: **Matching Signal Words With Answers**

The answers to some questions have many of the same words as what you heard or read. These are usually Knowledge questions. For example, if the story said, "A rat is on top of a hill" and the question is, "Where is the rat?" the answer would be, "The rat is on top of the hill."

Some signal words ask you to use your own words. These are usually Comprehension or Application questions. For example, if the story said, "I can pass you on the hill," said Al, and the question is "Explain what Al is doing," the answer could be, "Al is racing up the hill."

If the questions ask you to use the same words in your answer, mark a **K** for Knowledge in the "Same Words" column. If the questions asks you to use your own words in the answer, mark **C** for Comprehension or an **A** for Application in the "Own Words" column.

Same Words	Own Words	
		1. Which of Tam's parents had the day off?
		2. Can you think of anything a grown-up ever taught you? Describe the lessons.
		3. Make a list of the things they took to the beach.
		4. Predict what will happen next in the story.
		5. Where did he decide to take the family?

SPELLING

Student Mastery Score	Minimum Mastery Score	Maximum Mastery Score
	16	**20**
80% or more correct, progress to next Task.		

TASK 4: **Sentence Dictation**

Listen to the sentences your teacher says. Write the sentence that you hear. Check your spelling of new words from Unit 12. Remember, spelling counts only for words you have already learned.

1. _____

2. _____

3. _____

4. _____

5. _____

6. _____

7. _____

8. _____

9. _____

10. _____

11. _____

12. _____

13. _____

14. _____

15. _____

16. _____

17. _____

18. _____

19. _____

20. _____

Student Mastery Score	Minimum Mastery Score	Maximum Mastery Score
	45	56
80% or more correct, progress to next Task.		

TASK 5: Spelling Review

A. Spell the words your teacher says from Units 7-12. Check your own work.

1. _____   2. _____   3. _____   4. _____

5. _____   6. _____   7. _____   8. _____

9. _____   10. _____   11. _____   12. _____

13. _____   14. _____   15. _____   16. _____

17. _____   18. _____   19. _____   20. _____

21. _____   22. _____   23. _____   24. _____

25. _____   26. _____   27. _____   28. _____

29. _____   30. _____   31. _____   32. _____

33. _____   34. _____   35. _____   36. _____

37. _____   38. _____   39. _____   40. _____

41. _____   42. _____   43. _____   44. _____

45. _____   46. _____   47. _____   48. _____

B. Circle the words that you missed, so that you can practice them.

C. In the following blanks, write the words that are hardest for you to remember.

49. _____ 50. _____ 51. _____ 52. _____

53. _____ 54. _____ 55. _____ 56. _____

Student Mastery Score	Minimum Mastery Score	Maximum Mastery Score
	17	21
80% or more correct, progress to next Task.		

TASK 6: **Spelling Word List**

Write the words that your teacher dictates on the Spelling Practice forms in the back of this book.

Student Mastery Score	Minimum Mastery Score	Maximum Mastery Score
	4	5
80% or more correct, progress to next Task.		

TASK 7: **Spelling Mastery Sentences**

1. _____

2. _____

3. _____

4. _____

5. _____

WRITING

TASK 8: **Punctuation**

Student Mastery Score	Minimum Mastery Score	Maximum Mastery Score
	4	5
80% or more correct, progress to next Task.		

On the line under each sentence, rewrite the sentence using capital letters, periods, and question marks.

1. i wish that we could have met in new york

2. should they have the shells that we got in hong kong

3. i would have the vet, bill paswell, look at the dog's leg

4. have you put the things in the back of the pick-up

5. when can the gang help you with the project

ENGLISH/LANGUAGE ARTS

TASK 9: **Common Nouns and Proper Nouns**

Student Mastery Score	Minimum Mastery Score	Maximum Mastery Score
	6	8
80% or more correct, progress to next Task.		

Proper nouns name a particular person, place, or thing. Proper nouns begin with capital letters. All other nouns are common nouns. In the following, underline the first letter of each word that is a proper noun.

shell	new york	dish	miss america
mr. hill	store	sally	computer
ted bell	man	school	macmillan
bell	hill street school	contest	olympics

Student Mastery Score	Minimum Mastery Score	Maximum Mastery Score
	3	4
80% or more correct, progress to next Task.		

TASK 10: **Nouns and Verbs**

Some verbs can also be used as nouns. In the following sentences, some verbs are underlined. On the blank below each sentence, write a new sentence using the underlined verb as a subject (noun).

1. The little boy tried to <u>pet</u> the dog.

   _____

2. I <u>set</u> the table before we ate dinner.

   _____

3. Ken would <u>yell</u> in the window to see if they were at home.

   _____

4. His dad <u>bet</u> that we could not get back in time for the game.

   _____

Student Mastery Score	Minimum Mastery Score	Maximum Mastery Score
	12	15
80% or more correct, progress to next Task.		

TASK 11: **Words and Meanings**

Use a thesaurus to find three words or phrases that mean the same thing as the following words.

1. pen _____

2. doll _____

3. mess _____

4. let _____

5. leg _____

Student Mastery Score	Minimum Mastery Score	Maximum Mastery Score
	8	10
80% or more correct, progress to next Task.		

TASK 12: **Idioms**

Words that do not mean exactly what they say are called idioms. Explain the meaning of each idiom.

1. I fixed him up.

_____

2. quick-tempered

_____

3. dog-eared

_____

4. underdog

_____

5. hit it off

_____

6. ripped off

_____

7. give me a ring

_____

8. wishful thinking

_____

9. when pigs fly

_____

10. on his last leg

_____

Student Mastery Score	Minimum Mastery Score	Maximum Mastery Score
	8	**10**
80% or more correct, progress to next Task.		

TASK 13: **Suffixes**

We will read each of the following sentences aloud. Think about the correct suffix for the word in each. Then, write the correct word in the blank. Remember:

Add **-'s** to mean singular ownership.

Add **-s'** to mean plural ownership.

Add **-s** or **-es** to mean more than one (plural).

Add **-ing** to mean present time.

Add **-ed** to mean past time.

1. (Ben's, Bens') _____ glasses got lost.

2. Six of the (kid's, kids') _____ backpacks are missing.

3. We had ten (myths, myth's) _____ for English class.

4. Pat and Tam have fed the (pets, pet's) _____ .

5. Beth is standing on the (ships, ship's) _____ deck.

6. Ben and Jeff led the (races, race's) _____ last Saturday.

7. "Mom (begs, beg's) _____ Tom to help," said Sam.

8. The kids are (getting, gets) _____ the tests checked at the desk.

9. A red hen (pecks, peck's) _____ at the shed.

10. The (bell's, bells') _____ gong is ringing.

Spelling Practice

Name_____

Spell each reading and spelling vocabulary word correctly as your teacher reads it to you. Your teacher **will not score** the one word that you have crossed out.

1. _____
2. _____
3. _____
4. _____
5. _____
6. _____
7. _____
8. _____
9. _____
10. _____
11. _____
12. _____
13. _____
14. _____
15. _____
16. _____
17. _____
18. _____
19. _____
20. _____
21. _____
22. _____
23. _____
24. _____
25. _____
26. _____
27. _____
28. _____
29. _____
30. _____

Unit 7 spelling practice score: _____

Spelling Practice

Name_____

Spell each reading and spelling vocabulary word correctly as your teacher reads it to you. Your teacher **will not score** the one word that you have crossed out.

1. _____   2. _____

3. _____   4. _____

5. _____   6. _____

7. _____   8. _____

9. _____   10. _____

11. _____   12. _____

13. _____   14. _____

15. _____   16. _____

17. _____   18. _____

19. _____   20. _____

21. _____   22. _____

23. _____   24. _____

25. _____   26. _____

27. _____   28. _____

29. _____   30. _____

Unit 8 spelling practice score: _____

Spelling Practice

Name_____

Spell each reading and spelling vocabulary word correctly as your teacher reads it to you. Your teacher **will not score** the one word that you have crossed out.

1. _____   2. _____

3. _____   4. _____

5. _____   6. _____

7. _____   8. _____

9. _____   10. _____

11. _____   12. _____

13. _____   14. _____

15. _____   16. _____

17. _____   18. _____

19. _____   20. _____

21. _____   22. _____

23. _____   24. _____

25. _____   26. _____

27. _____   28. _____

29. _____   30. _____

Unit 9 spelling practice score: _____

Spelling Practice

Name _____

Spell each reading and spelling vocabulary word correctly as your teacher reads it to you. Your teacher **will not score** the one word that you have crossed out.

1. _____
2. _____
3. _____
4. _____
5. _____
6. _____
7. _____
8. _____
9. _____
10. _____
11. _____
12. _____
13. _____
14. _____
15. _____
16. _____
17. _____
18. _____
19. _____
20. _____
21. _____
22. _____
23. _____
24. _____
25. _____
26. _____
27. _____
28. _____
29. _____
30. _____

Unit 10 spelling practice score: _____

Spelling Practice

Name_____

Spell each reading and spelling vocabulary word correctly as your teacher reads it to you. Your teacher **will not score** the one word that you have crossed out.

1. _____   2. _____

3. _____   4. _____

5. _____   6. _____

7. _____   8. _____

9. _____   10. _____

11. _____   12. _____

13. _____   14. _____

15. _____   16. _____

17. _____   18. _____

19. _____   20. _____

21. _____   22. _____

23. _____   24. _____

25. _____   26. _____

27. _____   28. _____

29. _____   30. _____

Unit 11 spelling practice score: _____

Spelling Practice

Name_____

Spell each reading and spelling vocabulary word correctly as your teacher reads it to you. Your teacher **will not score** the one word that you have crossed out.

1. _____
2. _____
3. _____
4. _____
5. _____
6. _____
7. _____
8. _____
9. _____
10. _____
11. _____
12. _____
13. _____
14. _____
15. _____
16. _____
17. _____
18. _____
19. _____
20. _____
21. _____
22. _____
23. _____
24. _____
25. _____
26. _____
27. _____
28. _____
29. _____
30. _____

Unit 12 spelling practice score: _____